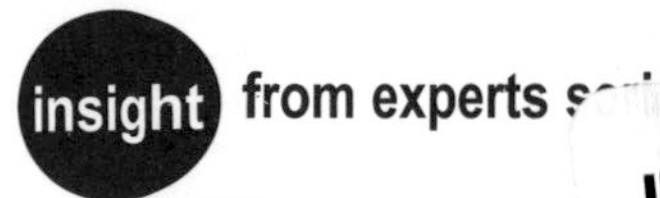

303 Solutions *for* Reaching Goals & Living Your Dreams

Compiled by

Doug Smart

Book Designer: Paula Chance

Disclaimer: This book is a compilation of ideas from numerous experts.
As such, the views expressed are those of the authors
and not necessarily the views of James & Brookfield Publishers.

For more information, contact:
James & Brookfield Publishers
P.O. Box 768024
Roswell, GA 30076

ISBN 0-9771912-3-0
Library of Congress Cataloging in Publication Data
10 9 8 7 6 5 4 3 2 1

"What you get by achieving your goals is not as important as what you become by achieving your goals."

— Zig Ziglar

1. **Give yourself permission to dream.**

– Robert Stack

2. Too few people ever write out personal goals, though many wonder why their lives don't turn out better. **Spend 60 minutes writing down your dreams and personal goals.** This exercise increases your chances by fifty percent of positive things happening that favor your goals, even if you never look at the paper again!

– Linda Edgecombe

3. **Stop dreaming about your goals and shift your focus to making your dreams come true.** Dreaming is often associated with sleeping. Wake up and make your dream a reality!

– Kafi Matimiloju

4. **I can think of a hundred reasons to not take a risk.** But that doesn't mean it is in my best interest to play it safe.

– Sid Ridgley

5. **Let your dreams grow into visions.** What's the difference? A dream is what you are able to see in your mind, as clearly as with physical eyes. A vision is the manifestation of the steps in order to make those dreams come true.

– Keith L. Brown

6. **Keep your work environment challenging, exciting, and rewarding.**

– Greg Maciolek

7. **You can create phenomenal power in your life by concentrating all your energies on a limited set of targets.**

– Mike Monahan

8. **Be excited!** People want to help enthusiastic and confident individuals. For example, many mentors say the enthusiasm and commitment of their mentees motivates them to want to do more to help. Excitement and enthusiasm are driving forces. Drive yourself to success!

– Donna Satchell

9. **If you have no plan, you are disconnected from your purpose.** In order to reach a goal you need a plan. Without a plan, your life is like a rudderless sailboat on the ocean, going whichever way the wind blows that day.

– David G. Lewis

10. **Use the "Magic of 3" by asking yourself the question, "What 3 things can I do today to move toward my goals?"** Then do not let anything deter you from doing those three things each day.

– Cheryl Stock

11. No one succeeds alone. **Send one handwritten thank-you note each day to someone who's invaluable to you.** Consider clients, vendors, coworkers, friends, and loved ones. The list can be as endless as your gratitude.

– Mandi Stanley

12. **Be bold and declare yourself the prime mover in your success.** With such a declaration, you will find the courage to fulfill your dreams.

– Phoebe Bailey

13. **Bring more brains into the game.** Create an open environment so people feel free to be candid and reveal the real truth, instead of being courteously remote.

– Connie Dieken

14. **Three Keys for Reaching Your Goals**

1. Know specifically what you want (see it)
2. Want it with all your heart (feel it)
3. Act as if you already have it (believe it)

– DJ Harrington

15. **If you truly commit to a plan, you only have to commit once.**

– Doug Smart

16. **By knowing precisely what you want to achieve, it gets easier for you to distinguish between the things that must be addressed from those that are distractions.** People without goals, although busy, allow much of their lives to be frittered away by the distractions.

– *Mike Monahan*

17. **Treat your time as if it was as valuable as money.** Reaching your goals is going to take lots of time and energy. Watch how you spend your time. It is an indication of how important you think your dream is.

– *Donna Satchell*

18. **The dream or vision that you commit to has to be the thing you want more than anything else.**

– Phoebe Bailey

19. **Visualize your goals.**

– Robert Stack

20. **Goals are the road map one uses to reach a particular destination.** Living a life without setting goals is like leaving home heading to an unknown or unfamiliar destination without a map.

– David G. Lewis

21. **Keep your goals visible.** Post them near your computer where you'll see them every day. Visuals are "stickier" than thoughts and words and prompt quicker results.

– Connie Dieken

22. **Limit the number of goals you work on at one time.** A lot of people don't achieve their goals because they want everything at once. Tackling them one at a time makes it easier to accomplish. Once you accomplish the first one, move onto the second goal, then the third. This will build your momentum as you develop confidence, contacts, and systems that will make achieving further goals easier.

– Cheryl Stock

23. **Set aside time and plan for your best future.** Many people put more effort into planning a party than planning their business or professional goals. Use the same enthusiasm and diligence to plan your personal and professional goals and your reward will be a life-long party.

– Kafi Matimiloju

24. **Life is a mystery to be lived, not a problem to be solved.**

– Sid Ridgley

25. **Many of us fail to write out our goals thinking we risk feeling like "losers" because others will see if we are unable to fulfill our goals.** But the reality is, if we realized how little others think about us, we'd stop worrying about it and just get on with living the lives we want.

– Linda Edgecombe

26. **Focus on the one thing you can control: yourself.** Never stop learning and dreaming until they plant you.

– Greg Maciolek

27. **When someone pays you a compliment, respect their good judgment by saying, "thank you."**

– Mandi Stanley

28. **If you don't take time to smell the roses you will sooner be buried under them.**

– DJ Harrington

29. Stop taking advice from the dream killers! **Never let anyone tell you what you cannot do, especially if they have never done it.**

– Keith L. Brown

30. **Dreams are wishes. Goals are destinations.**

– Doug Smart

31. **Goals help you get what you want, rather than having to settle for what you might end up with.**

– Mike Monahan

32. **Don't *depend* on the outcome of any one goal.** Have multiple goals in play.

– Robert Stack

33. **Life is a series of obstacles.** Don't let failures overwhelm you. In order to win, you have to be OK with losing (every once in a while)!

– David G. Lewis

34. **Make sure your goals meet the BAM criteria. They must be *believable*, *achievable* and *measurable*.**

– Cheryl Stock

35. **Stop dreaming and start doing!** Don't get stuck on the wrong side of achieving your goals. Dreaming will give you hope, but having a plan and putting action into your dream will create results!

– Kafi Matimiloju

36. **Start smart by beginning with a goal in mind.**

– Robert Stack

37. **Work exceedingly well with others.** George Frazier noted, "All of life is about working with and through other people. There is no success that you can attain, sustain, or maintain on your own, by yourself or in a vacuum. All successful people have mastered this skill."

– Donna Satchell

38. **Here is a goal that will make it easier to reach your other goals: make the best use of valuable time and make better decisions faster.**

– Greg Maciolek

39. **Read. Read. Read.** Set a book-reading goal, and keep track of it. Each year I set a goal of reading 50 books on a wealth of topics. I keep a "books-I-have-read" list in my briefcase. At the end of the year, it's wonderful to review the list to remind myself of the ideas and lessons I've learned as a result. Nothing expands my mind or contributes to my professional development more.

– Mandi Stanley

40. **Change creates new roads to success.**

– DJ Harrington

41. Though vision is yours, there are many ways to reach the goal. **Brainstorm with others.**

– Phoebe Bailey

42. **Don't moan about work-life balance.** Balance means making choices and implementing them. Only you know the trade-offs you're willing to make. Clarify the outcomes you want and say "no" to things that don't fit.

– Connie Dieken

43. **Do what serves you.**

– Robert Stack

44. **You can't live a maximum wage life with a minimum wage attitude!**

– Keith L. Brown

45. **Scenario planning is a great way to minimize risk.** What is the best case scenario? Worst case? Most likely case?

– Sid Ridgley

46. **Life's number one goal is *happiness*.**

– Linda Edgecombe

47. **Life's number two goal is *to know that you can leave this world with as few regrets as possible*.** So make a list of all the things you want to get done and start working on them. Today!

– Linda Edgecombe

48. **Ask for help.** No matter what you want to accomplish, you cannot do it all by yourself. A survey by Office Team, a leading staffing service, found that the number one mistake people make in networking is not asking for help. Many people underutilize their network of support. Keep in mind that asking for help means being willing to accept "no" while being open to the possibility of hearing "yes."

– Donna Satchell

49. **Telling the truth is always the less risky path.**

– Sid Ridgley

50. **Straight talk and more of it.** Most visions and values are just hot air. Tie your goals to real actions so you'll know when you've reached them.

– *Connie Dieken*

51. **Remember the art of the thank-you note, especially when others help you reach important goals.** It's thoughtful, quick, and easy with *TBA*:

- *Thank* them for the gift or service
- State one tangible *benefit* you received
- Tell them what you *appreciate* about it and their thoughtfulness

– *Mandi Stanley*

52. **The best fruit is never close to the ground.** Get comfortable taking more risks.

– DJ Harrington

53. **When you find yourself procrastinating, running into obstacles or getting sidetracked from your goals, ask yourself "what should I be doing, what should I not be doing and what should I be doing next?" to get back on track.**

– Cheryl Stock

54. **Avoid pigeonholing yourself and others.** This is a sure way to stifle talent.

– Phoebe Bailey

55. **Take control of your goals and dreams by becoming the CEO of your life.** Chief Operating Officers are responsible for achieving profit, success, and excellence for their employees and shareholders. As the CEO of your life, you are responsible for achieving the same results for your "investors," too. Think and act like a CEO and build profit, success and excellence for your own life and those closest to you.

– *Kafi Matimiloju*

56. **You can have anything you want in life if you want it bad enough and if you are willing to pay the price.** Almost always, the price is measured in emotion, not money.

– *Doug Smart*

57. Our youth has coined a word, *crunk*. It means to get excited about a particular song, event, or life in general. When it comes to your goals and aspirations, get "crunk," which I see standing for ***consciously receive undertakings of new knowledge***.

– Keith L. Brown

58. **Goal setting gives you long-term vision and short-term motivation.** It focuses your acquisition of knowledge and helps you organize your resources.

– Mike Monahan

59. Deep motivation does not come from reading this book or listening to speakers. **Motivation comes from movement.**

– Linda Edgecombe

60. **Use your "creative powers" to create positive environments for others.** For example, if you are someone else's boss, create a better work environment for your employees. If you are a parent, create an environment that inspires your child to explore and dream of becoming the best he or she can be.

– Greg Maciolek

61. **Keep your goals in front of you.** The busyness of your life can detour your focus onto activities unrelated to your goals. But having your goals in front of you, such as in your daily planner, on scheduling software, or on a bulletin board can help you choose daily activities that will lead to goal achievement.

– Mike Monahan

62. **Clarity in communication can transform lofty goals into reachable goals.**

– Connie Dieken

63. **Live your life to the brim.** Make your life good to the last drop by setting goals. In order to get the most out of your life you have to challenge yourself to do more, be more and get more than you did the day before!

– David G. Lewis

64. **Speak in terms of challenges, not problems.** Challenges are solvable. Problems are burdensome. If you call your challenges problems you further burden yourself. I quit using the word problems over fifteen years ago.

– Doug Smart

65. **Progress without risk equals *status quo*.**

– Sid Ridgley

66. Staffing is crucial to the vision. **Surround yourself with people who will help you achieve your vision.**

– Greg Maciolek

67. **Surround yourself with people who care about you.**

– David G. Lewis

68. **Ask two people to mentor you.** One should be in your profession and the other outside of it. Both should be considerably more successful than you.

– Doug Smart

69. **Don't be so independent as to think you do not need help in reaching your goals.** If Tiger Woods, with so much natural talent, needs a coach to help him improve his golf swing, then the rest of us surely can make use of a coach too!

– Greg Maciolek

70. **If you are reading this book, you have it better than ninety-eight percent of the population of the planet.**

– DJ Harrington

71. **Be helpful to others.** According to the law of karma, when we assist others, that same energy of support is returned to us. Interestingly, many times our help comes from someone other than the person we assist.

– Donna Satchell

72. **Expect to give as much as or more than you expect to get.**

– Mandi Stanley

73. **If you are having problems achieving your goals, check your commitment by asking yourself "Where is my body right now?"** Where your body is reflects your commitment. For example, if you want to lose weight but haven't been able, ask yourself the "where is my body" question. If the answer is "on the couch snacking and watching television," you realize the incongruence between behavior and commitment. Once you spot that, it is easier to regain control and get back on track by quickly changing to a behavior that will help you succeed.

– Cheryl Stock

74. **Fear of success holds many of us back.** The fear is that after reaching goals we are left to wonder "Now what?" The answer is that goal posts need to be set out a bit farther, which means we need to stretch.

– Linda Edgecombe

75. **If self-doubt stops your commitment cold in its tracks, follow Goethe's advice: "Whatever you can do or dream, begin it. Boldness has genius, power and magic in it."**

– Phoebe Bailey

76. **Put one foot in front of the other and start on your goals.** That's when the magic happens. It will simply unfold and, almost magically, the quickness with which you get close to your goals may surprise you.

– Linda Edgecombe

77. **Plan with passion, execute with enthusiasm.**

– Kafi Matimiloju

78. **Rev your engine.** Clarify your goals down to the nitty-gritty to ensure your business runs more efficiently in every way.

– Connie Dieken

79. **Dream big for your future and release the nightmares of your past.** My pastor, Gary Taylor, said to the parishioners, "Your memory is a re-play of your past, but your imagination is a pre-play of your future! Imagine the possibilities!"

– *Keith L. Brown*

80. **Understand that strength grows out of struggle.**

– *David G. Lewis*

81. **Here is a very simple technique for reaching your goals and living your dreams: *show up early.***

– *Mandi Stanley*

82. **Stretching to reach goals takes energy.** When compared to doing nothing or very little, you can see that many people take the path of least resistance by rationalizing, "It's not so bad the way it is." They may not like their present circumstances but they are content to accept them.

– Linda Edgecombe

83. **Playing it safe is also a risky choice.**

– Sid Ridgley

84. **If you think it, you will intend it.** Intentions lead to actions. Actions craft our lives.

– Robert Stack

85. **A goal should be flexible.** If conditions should change for reasons outside your control, you should re-examine your goal rather than cling stubbornly to something that is no longer realistic. The situation may call for either an upward or downward adjustment.

– Mike Monahan

86. **Avoid the naysayers.** Those who belittle your successes, avoid them like the plague. They are as deadly as a plague because they drain you of your confidence, commitment, joy, and enthusiasm, the very things you will need for reaching higher goals.

– Donna Satchell

87. **If you decide to share or take on the goals of others, such as at work, look for ways they can reflect your personality and meet your needs, too, otherwise your energy and enthusiasm will wane.**

– Kafi Matimiloju

88. If you want to earn more, learn more. **Be a perpetual student.**

– DJ Harrington

89. **Become friends with people who are successful in the way you want to be successful.** For example, if you want to be rich, hang out with rich people. Observe how they think and act. You cannot get this information from books.

– Doug Smart

90. **Get a dream team to help you.** Identify several people who can help you turn your dreams into action. Ask for support and help. If you are sincere in wanting to achieve your dreams, you will find most people happy to help you.

– Cheryl Stock

91. **Keep dreams enticing by organizing a journey of small steps.** Completion of these will stimulate you toward completion of your biggest dreams.

– Phoebe Bailey

92. **Give yourself permission to be great.** It's what you think that counts. To achieve your goals, you first have to be mentally prepared for success. If you're not, you'll sabotage yourself with guilt and feeling unworthy.

– Connie Dieken

93. **Turn your negative self-talk from "What if I don't?" to "What if I do?"** Stop talking yourself out of your own success — there are enough jealous people around already doing that for you. Don't waste your time and energy destroying yourself, instead, use your inner thoughts to build your confidence and take yourself to the top of your game.

– Kafi Matimiloju

94. **Stay away from negative people.** They will never get the picture, because they're in the wrong frame of mind. Take these negatives and symbolically place them in a dark room, hoping they will develop. Get away from them in a flash, so you can become the empowered exposure you were created to be!

– Keith L. Brown

95. **Know that there are people out there who share your dreams. Find them and work with them.**

– Phoebe Bailey

96. **Join associations that focus on your endeavors.** If your goal is to be a painter, join an association of artists. If your goal is to write a novel, join an association of writers. By association, you learn, grow, and develop relationships that can help you move forward.

– Donna Satchell

97. **Associate with people of integrity, honesty and creativity and you will build exponential synergy.**

– DJ Harrington

98. **A goal must be demanding in order to motivate you to do your best.** Don't make your goals too easy; you'll cheat yourself.

– Mike Monahan

99. Here is an affirmation worth repeating daily, "When it comes to my dreams, goals, and vision, I have two options. Either I'm going to make it or **I'M GOING TO MAKE IT!**"

– Keith L. Brown

100. **Make goals concrete.** Avoid long, drawn-out descriptions of lofty goals and visions. Instead, stick to clear language that describes a tangible, concrete plan of action.

– Connie Dieken

101. **Never think or say this again: "If I can't do it well, then I won't do it at all."** Who, quite frankly, cares whether you are the best at something or not? That is so not the point! The point is to get started. Now!

– Linda Edgecombe

102. **Strive for excellence, not perfection.** Perfectionism can hold you a prisoner and can keep you from your dreams.

– Cheryl Stock

103. With your goal or mission in mind, write down your responses to this fill-in-the-blank opener: "The biggest challenges I have before me right now are _______." **Naming your challenges is a very important first step to overcoming them.**

– Mandi Stanley

104. Take stock of where you are now. Compare that to where you want to be. **You will get a pretty good idea of what you need to do to close the gap.**

– Greg Maciolek

105. **By writing your goals, you increase your chances of doing something about them by about fifty percent.** You awaken your "Reticular Activating System."

– Linda Edgecombe

106. **Every "win" you have had in life involved taking a risk.**

– Sid Ridgley

107. **Align your actions with your personal values as the surest path to achieving your dreams.**

– Robert Stack

108. **Caution! Share your goals and dreams with supporters not destroyers.** Share your dreams, goals, and ambitions with those who will support you. Naysayers will find fault in what you are trying to achieve and may try to destroy your vision.

– Kafi Matimiloju

109. **Review, streamline and prioritize "to do" lists at the end of each day.** Do not be afraid to remove something that once seemed a good idea.

– Phoebe Bailey

110. **Decide what results you want from your life.** Minimum investments will yield minimum returns. Maximum investments can yield maximum returns. You make the call.

– David G. Lewis

111. **You can set your goals for your wants or your needs.** Your wants are your dreams, so those are higher goals.

– DJ Harrington

112. **Be willing to change your thinking in order to get new results.** This can mean doing things in different ways and changing how you treat others.

– Donna Satchell

113. **Establish your "dream cocktail."** Take your definition of success; add some passion, a dose of excitement and a pinch of challenge. Mix well and serve over life.

– Kafi Matimiloju

114. **Breakthroughs happen when people challenge established "norms."** For example, Roger Banister believed he could run one mile in under four minutes, although the wisdom of the day considered that an impossibility. What is even more astounding than Banister's success in breaking the barrier is the fact that the following year 236 other runners broke it, too.

– Doug Smart

115. **Purify complicated goals.** Strip away clutter that doesn't contribute to a positive outcome.

– Connie Dieken

116. **Fear is not the signal to stop.** It is your opportunity to strengthen your courage.

– Phoebe Bailey

117. **When you are feeling overwhelmed, clean out a drawer!** Tackle a desk drawer, file drawer, kitchen drawer or bathroom drawer. The process of organization helps your brain regain focus. This will help you clear and reclaim control of your thinking. It will be easier to get back on track to taking action steps that will help you reach your goal.

– Cheryl Stock

118. Most of us are hard-wired to avoid the emotion of guilt. **We'd rather not write out our goals then risk thinking, "I'll feel guilty if I don't reach them."**

– Linda Edgecombe

119. **Empower people as a means for helping your customers reach their goals.**
Empowerment is giving people the authority to act in the best interests of your customers.

– Sid Ridgley

120. **Empowerment without accountability results in poor decisions and poor results.**

– Sid Ridgley

121. **It's goal setting not goal sitting!**

– Keith L. Brown

122. **Know yourself.**

– Robert Stack

123. **Every single day is a fresh start on success.**

– DJ Harrington

124. **What you do today, multiplied by time, will determine what you are able to do five years from now.**

– David G. Lewis

125. **Start everyday with a prioritized "to do" list.** Reaching your goals takes focus. Focus comes from knowing exactly what you need to do at any given time of the day. Discipline yourself to prioritize your tasks, making the most important activities the first to get done.

– Donna Satchell

126. **Have a good handshake that shows people you are on your way.** Don't ever be accused of having the "dead fish," "limp noodle," "death grip," "knuckler," or "lobster pincher" handshake. Instead, master the art of the "equality" handshake. The webbed, fleshy part between your thumb and forefinger should connect with the other person's. Have a nice, firm grip. Give one to two pumps. Then, exit the handshake. Don't overdo it.

– Mandi Stanley

127. **A goal must be specific and measurable.** If your goal is vague and nonspecific, how will you know when you have achieved it? Here are some examples. "Spend more time with my family" is not an adequate goal. However, the goal, "Be home in time for supper four nights during the week" is very specific. "Increase sales" is not as good as "increase sales by 15% over last year." With measurable goals like this, you have something concrete to shoot for and will know if you succeed or not.

– Mike Monahan

128. **Your work environment must nourish the vision, with an environment or culture where people are respected and heard.**

– Greg Maciolek

129. **I always say, "Dreams and drama do not mix."** Minimize the personal drama in your life so you can focus your time and energy on making your dreams a reality.

– Donna Satchell

130. **Die for your dreams: *delight*, *ignite*, and *excite* daily.**

– Keith L. Brown

131. **Become the MVP (Most Valuable Player) of your own Super Bowl.** Don't just watch from the stands. Participate and play in the game — for this Super Bowl is the game that represents your life.

– Kafi Matimiloju

132. **Change your attitude, change your behavior.** New behaviors lead to new actions. It's that simple—and that complex.

– Connie Dieken

133. **Surround yourself with people who expect more of you than you expect of yourself.**

– Phoebe Bailey

134. **Give yourself more time to get the right things done.** For example, move your "in box" away from your desktop. This encourages you to take one "in box" item at a time. Dealing with each one with intention helps with concentration so you can make faster decisions and get them all done more readily.

– Cheryl Stock

135. **It's not what you work on that matters, it is what you accomplish.** It is possible to be too busy to be goal oriented. You want to be so goal oriented that you don't give up valuable time to busyness.

– Doug Smart

136. **A sure way to reach your goals is to help others reach theirs.**

– DJ Harrington

137. **Don't give away your advantage by comparing yourself to others.** The sooner you identify your special gifts and talents, the sooner you can reach your goals.

– David G. Lewis

138. **Leave every place and every situation a little better than you found it.**

– Mandi Stanley

139. **Don't resignedly accept your "station" in life.** I've witnessed too many people living their parent's dream or not realizing that they were capable of much more.

– Greg Maciolek

140. Identify what is most important to you by identifying twenty values. Then, prioritize and pare that list to your top five. **Set goals and make your daily decisions on those five core values.** This will help you reach your goals and live a balanced life.

– Linda Edgecombe

141. **Gain a rich insight about yourself in only a few minutes by making a list of your life-long dreams, desires and goals.** Think like a thirteen-year-old. That is, suspend logic or worries about ability, money or logistics. Make a list of at least fifty. Group around common themes. Compare these to your five top values. Then answer this for each group: "This is important to me because_____." Add action steps to your calendar for the next twelve months, including scheduling something significant you will accomplish on one of your goals in the next fifteen days. Take this deeper by further identifying a specific action you will take on this particular goal within three days. Email me or a friend to proclaim what you are going to do. This establishes accountability. Odds are, you will reach your goal!

– Linda Edgecombe

142. **Preparation builds confidence.**

– Sid Ridgley

143. **We all have the power to dream.**

– Robert Stack

144. **A goal should be written and displayed where you will be reminded of it often.** If not, it is too easily forgotten. If you try to retain it in your mind, it may change every time you think about it, making it a less steady target.

– Mike Monahan

145. **Evaluate your skills and abilities to identify areas in which you need to improve.** Plan to take classes, read books, get professional assistance, or advice to grow and develop in areas you are lacking in some way.

– Donna Satchell

146. "Perfection" does not exist! It never has, and never will! Get it? Good! **And now go and try something you've always wanted to try without fear that you won't do a perfect job of it.**

– Linda Edgecombe

147. When I've asked people who obviously hated their jobs, "Why don't you do something else?" They usually answer similar to this: "I have a spouse, two kids and don't have enough time to work on any goals." Yet when I ask them how many sports leagues they are involved with, they typically answer, "three or four!" They have time to play sports but never the time to better themselves. **People will let self-imposed barriers block them from getting what they say they want.**

– Greg Maciolek

148. **Stay focused.** Keep your eyes on the prize, in spite of what is taking place on the sidelines.

– David G. Lewis

149. Don't let disorganization blur your focus. **At home, organize in 3's—one pile to throw away, one pile to give to someone else (charity shops, family members, or send to the cleaners), and the third pile to keep.** Clean your closets this way, your piles of paper, your garage, and any "stuff" that has accumulated and is unruly.

– Cheryl Stock

150. **Stop "starting and stopping."** Go full-speed ahead and resist the urge to put your goals on the backburner while something else takes priority.

– Connie Dieken

151. **Develop a timeline for achieving your goal.** Define what you want to achieve and by when. Your timeline should clearly state what you want to accomplish or be by a specific date. Make it happen.

– Kafi Matimiloju

152. **Your dreams should include multiple streams (of income).** Many people are complaining about their income. Inside of you are gifts you are hiding from the world. Take that wrapping paper off! Sure, it's good to look at, but it has no value because the gift is on the inside. Don't allow your income to determine your outcome! You can enhance your income and increase your value. How? Invest in your dreams. I was an educator and part-time speaker before I launched a full time speaking career. If your gross pay is gross and your net has you trapped in a net of despair, use your genuine gift (often a hobby) to get paid what you deserve. For instance, if you're an educator with a great singing voice, earn extra income by singing at weddings and other events. If you're a cashier who bakes delicious desserts, market those desserts during the holiday season. Stop complaining and start doing. If you complain, you will remain!

– Keith L. Brown

153. **You cannot make anybody do anything, but you can influence them to want to help you reach your goals.**

– Doug Smart

154. **Dreams are kept alive through sharing.**

– Phoebe Bailey

155. **Admit what you don't know.**

– Robert Stack

156. **When it comes to things that matter the most to you, make your enthusiasm contagious.**

– DJ Harrington

157. General Colin Powell's definition of success really resonates with me. He described success this way, **"In one word—generosity. Give of yourself, your talents, your contacts, and your hard work to make others successful in their endeavors, all without keeping score."**

– Mandi Stanley

158. **A goal must have a deadline.** Deadlines provide a sense of urgency and a way of tracking progress. A deadline creates the necessity for taking concrete action.

– Mike Monahan

159. **Thank the risk takers, for they make our lives richer.**

– Sid Ridgley

160. **Get comfortable with feeling uncomfortable.** Reaching your dreams is going to take doing activities that are outside of your comfort zone. It may be asking for help, giving a speech, attending networking events, or any number of activities. Take action despite discomfort. These challenging experiences will make you stronger.

– Donna Satchell

161. **Create a culture of high expectations and play full out.**

– Phoebe Bailey

162. **Take time each day to do something just for yourself.** This can be as simple as taking a few minutes to hum a favorite tune.

– Cheryl Stock

163. **Organize a daily schedule and stick to it.** This develops discipline, which is the first step towards reaching your goals.

– David G. Lewis

164. **Return all phone calls and answer all correspondence immediately.** This will save you time and energy, plus it will create goodwill and support amongst people who can help you.

– Mandi Stanley

165. **Make a life list of things you want to do before you checkout of this life.** Then work towards accomplishing them.

– Greg Maciolek

166. **Establish your "dream team."** When it comes to reaching your goals and living your dreams, it is important you form your own support network. Include friends, family members and associates who will make you accountable and support your goals.

– Kafi Matimiloju

167. **Communicate with yourself.** Be certain of the clarity and integrity of your message before you ask for buy-in from others.

– Connie Dieken

168. **Got a dream or a goal? Name it! Claim it! Frame it!**

– Keith L. Brown

169. We learn from two sources: experience and reading. The latter is much easier and a lot less painful. **Read everything you can about what you want to accomplish.** For example, if you want to run a restaurant, dive into reading about running restaurants. Absorbing lots of focused information will give you confidence, clarity, and credibility.

– Doug Smart

170. **School is never out for a pro.**

– DJ Harrington

171. **I can think of a hundred reasons to not take a risk.** But I choose to take risks, anyhow, in order to get what I want in life.

– Sid Ridgley

172. **Woody Allen said, "Eighty percent of success is just showing up."** Make sure you show up for networking events, organization meetings, volunteer activities and everything else you have committed to doing.

– Donna Satchell

173. Research indicates that when people are near the end of their lives, if they have any regrets at all, those tend to fall into two categories: regrets that they did not have better relationships with people they love and *regrets that they did not try.* **Avoid regrets by taking the risks necessary to get what you want in life.**

– Doug Smart

174. **Goals have a built-in call to action.** Write them with strong, clear phrases such as "I will fix ___", "I will obtain ____", "I will complete _____". The type of action you need to take should be clear from the way you state your goals.

– Mike Monahan

175. **The secret to success is not in building more buildings, but in building meaningful relationships.**

– David G. Lewis

176. **When you finish reading a good book, ask this question: "What is one lesson I've learned from this book?" Or, "what is one great idea I can apply to my business, my life, or my relationships as a result of reading this book?"** The results can be life changing!

– Mandi Stanley

177. **You are a role model for your children.**

When you accept self-imposed barriers as excuses for not living your dreams, your children observe. This can plant seeds of doubt and limitation in their minds as to what they can accomplish.

– Greg Maciolek

178. **Define *your own* goals and dreams.**

Get involved in determining your future, otherwise others will plan and direct your life. Take responsibility for your success.

– Kafi Matimiloju

179. **I always say, "The disease to please will bury your dreams."** Avoid being a people pleaser. That is a sure way to not reach your goals. Do not fall victim to thinking you must make everyone happy. You cannot, and it is a misuse of the valuable time and energy you will need for reaching your goals.

– Donna Satchell

180. **Recipe to sabotage your goals: Hog conversations, take disproportionate credit for a team's success and sap other people's energy.**

– Connie Dieken

181. **Resist the impulse to stay in your comfort zone.** It is an impulse designed to maintain the status quo.

– Phoebe Bailey

182. **Use proper grammar.** Education and intelligence help garner the support of other educated and intelligent people.

– Mandi Stanley

183. **Learn and grow from each setback.**

– Robert Stack

184. **Persistence pays.** For example, it is a known fact that 80% of sales are made after the fifth contact, and yet a majority of salespeople stop after one. This dynamic applies to achieving goals as well. Many people simply quit too soon.

– Cheryl Stock

185. **Ambitious and measurable goals galvanize people and get them moving in the same direction.**

– Sid Ridgley

186. **A goal should be agreed to by those who must achieve it.** This will heighten their enthusiasm and commitment for successful outcomes. Without this sense of ownership, they will feel less driven by commitment then by obligation.

– Mike Monahan

187. **Being accountable to someone or a group of people is the most amazing and powerful tool for getting all the things you want in your life.** Create an accountability group of your own today.

– Linda Edgecombe

188. **Avoid negative thinking by staying positive.** It is very easy to slip into the trap of negative thinking when things are not going well. It can easily become a way of life that will hold you back. Positive thinking propels you forward.

– Donna Satchell

189. **It's not about you or me! It's about us.**

– David G. Lewis

190. When you were a kid, people asked you, "What do you want to be when you grow up?" **Are you living your answer?** What will it take?

– Keith L. Brown

191. **What you are going to do is far less important than what you are doing now and have done in the past.**

– DJ Harrington

192. Write down your dreams and goals. Keep them close at hand, by the phone, in your car, on your bathroom mirror. **Putting your goals on paper helps begin the process of making your dreams come true and then it re-enforces your power to make your dreams come true.**

– Cheryl Stock

193. **Release the need to be right.**

– Robert Stack

194. **Be humble in measuring your successes and compassionate in assessing your failures.**

– Phoebe Bailey

195. **Goal setting can go wrong for several reasons:**

- Goals can be set unrealistically high
- Goals can be set so low that you feel no challenge or benefit in achieving them
- Goals can be so vague that they are useless
- Goal setting can be unsystematic, sporadic, and disorganized
- You can have many goals that are not prioritized

– Mike Monahan

196. **Let the past reside in the past.** Focus on the present and the future. One of my favorite quotes is by Bryd Baggett: "Look at life through the windshield, not the rear-view mirror". It is hard to move forward if we are looking backwards.

– Donna Satchell

197. **Take the time to understand what you're going to do and how you're going to deal with the inevitable detours along the way.**

– Sid Ridgley

198. **Be congruent.** Make your words and your actions match. If they don't, your goals are just lip service.

– Connie Dieken

199. **Almost all barriers to growing and dreaming are self-imposed.** It is hard to grow if a person tells himself, "I can't." It makes me think of the old saying, "you can't get to second base if you never leave first base."

– Greg Maciolek

200. **Dream big and go for it!** What's the worse that can happen?

– Kafi Matimiloju

201. **Have faith.**

– Mandi Stanley

202. Choose to solve bigger problems. **It takes no more energy to solve a $5,000 problem then to solve a $50,000 problem.**

– Doug Smart

203. **Think big, think bold, think brilliant!** Breathe life into creating and defining your own goals, then make them as unique as you are.

– Kafi Matimiloju

204. **Stop caring if you do or don't *reach* your goals.** Having and striving for goals propels us. You will be pleasantly surprised to find how you gravitate toward your goals because you put them in writing and took action steps.

– Linda Edgecombe

205. **Who are we kidding? No one ever gets it right the first time!**

– Sid Ridgley

206. Switch your attitude from ***impossible*** **to** ***I'M POSSIBLE!***

– Keith L. Brown

207. **You own your dreams.**

– Robert Stack

208. **Allow your dreams to grow with you.** Your goals will change as you mature. Adjust them as needed and allow them to reflect the growth in your personality and lifestyle.

– Kafi Matimiloju

209. **If you are negative, unsure or pessimistic about goal achievement, your staff will feel the same way.** It is best to be positive, yet realistic.

– Greg Maciolek

210. **The first sale is always to yourself.** When you talk to yourself what do you say?

– David G. Lewis

211. **Relentless communication of goals is vital.** Repeating team goals over and over again is vital for accomplishing superior results.

– Connie Dieken

212. Stop asking children, "What do you want to be when you grow up?" Instead, ask, "What are you going to be in the future?" **Help people change from wishful thinking to empowered thinking.**

– Keith L. Brown

213. **Periodically review your progress towards your goals.** Feedback like this turns all experiences into positive learning opportunities. Even failing to meet a goal is a step forward toward high performance if you learn from it.

– Mike Monahan

214. **Don't ask poor people how to get rich.** Although well intentioned, they do not have the perspective of rich people.

– Doug Smart

215. **When your goals are consciously on your mind, you naturally recognize events and opportunities that help you reach your goals.**

– Linda Edgecombe

216. **Anchor your dreams to concrete actions and timelines.**

– Phoebe Bailey

217. **Learn from your failures and use the information to propel your success.** If you fail to achieve a goal, learn from the experience and move yourself onwards and upwards. Don't dwell on what went wrong, but use it to your advantage and take yourself to the top.

– Kafi Matimiloju

218. **Create a "treasure map" or "dream map" for reaching high achievements.** On a piece of cardboard, place a collage of pictures and photos representing your dreams. Hang it in a place where you can see it daily. This visual will fuel the process of manifesting your dreams. From personal experience I can happily say it works!

– Donna Satchell

219. Never forget that thoughts are powerful. **If you think you can, you have a better chance of doing it than if you say you will try.**

– Cheryl Stock

220. **Ponder less and implement more.** Grow and be better for the experience.

– Connie Dieken

221. **Having problems is not a problem.** The problem is when you have the same problem five years later. In that case, the problem is you because you have not changed enough to get past the problem.

– Doug Smart

222. **Grow into your goals by learning something new every day.**

– Robert Stack

223. **Every person who achieves greatness finds the strength to persist even when faced with setbacks and failures.**

– Sid Ridgley

224. **Just as thriving organizations have different levels of goals, to be a thriving individual you should have personal goals that are monthly, yearly, and life-time.**

– Greg Maciolek

225. **Designate a notebook for the exclusive recording or your goals. Otherwise they will evaporate along with the excitement that brought them.**

– Phoebe Bailey

226. **Your goals and dreams are not about what you think they are about, but you won't have the pleasure of finding that out until you are in the middle of going after them.**

– Linda Edgecombe

227. **Before you can reach your goals, you must reach for your goals!**

– Keith L. Brown

228. **If you do not reach a goal, ensure you learn the lessons of the failure:**

- That you didn't try hard enough
- That your technique, skills, or knowledge were faulty and need to be enhanced
- That the goal you set was unrealistic

– *Mike Monahan*

229. **Learn from your mistakes.** "Lessons" are the names we can give our mistakes when we choose to see life as a learning experience. When you make a mistake (and we all do), learn from the situation so you are more likely to be successful in the future.

– *Donna Satchell*

230. **Don't hide behind a firewall.** Be open to new ideas and forward-moving contributors.

– Connie Dieken

231. **Save time by being direct and not waiting to ask for what you want or need.**

– Sid Ridgley

232. **In order to live your dream, help others to live their dreams.**

– David G. Lewis

233. **Re-invest in your success by sharing it with others.** True quality of life is not about how much success you earn, it comes from how much of your success you share with others. As a successful person, you did not get to where you are by yourself. Give help and support to others pursing their dreams!

– Kafi Matimiloju

234. **Get a buddy — having someone to be accountable to can help you stay on track.**

– Cheryl Stock

235. **Pursuing your dreams will provide you with a soaring sense of freedom!** Not pursuing your dreams will provide you with the oppressive feeling of being trapped.

– Keith L. Brown

236. Take an inventory of your skills and experiences. **Determine your strengths and areas in need of development for achieving your dreams.** Then get to work.

– Phoebe Bailey

237. **It takes more energy to be poor than to be rich.**

– Doug Smart

238. **Set your goals to work for you, not against you.**

– DJ Harrington

239. **Be willing to serve as a resource for others even as you ask others to serve as a resource for you.**

– Mandi Stanley

240. **Be persistent.** Reaching your goals is not going to happen overnight or even over a few months. It may take years. But hang in there.

– Donna Satchell

241. **A well developed plan will help you keep the faith during difficult times.**

– Sid Ridgley

242. **Your degree of commitment will determine the degree of difficulty of the task.**

– David G. Lewis

243. **Reward yourself for the good things you do.** Remember the feelings. Replay them to get you through times that are not so good.

– DJ Harrington

244. You are a one-of-a-kind person. **To succeed as an entrepreneur, capitalize on how your unique qualities will help your customers reach their goals.**

– Doug Smart

245. **To reach your goals, you will need to learn to delegate as well as you possibly can.** You do not have the time or the talent to do everything yourself.

– Linda Edgecombe

246. **There are no shortcuts to reaching success.** The journey is often long and laborious. Stay on track and keep your goals in sight. Once you get there, it's worth it!

– Kafi Matimiloju

247. **When you achieve a goal, it should feed back into your next goals.**

- If the goal was easily achieved, make your next goals harder
- If the goal took a dispiriting length of time to achieve, make the next goal a little easier
- If you learned something that would lead you to change goals still outstanding, do so
- If while achieving the goal, you noticed a deficit in your skills, set goals to fix this

– Mike Monahan

248. **Your feelings reflect how you see the situation.**

– Robert Stack

249. For maximum effectiveness, goals must be written and reviewed often. Action plans must be created. **Otherwise, all you have is a mental list of good intentions.**

– Greg Maciolek

250. **If you find yourself off track while moving towards your goal, ask yourself the question, "what am I making more important than my goal?"**

– Cheryl Stock

251. **Nothing is better than a good night's rest for restoring your energy and clearing your mind.**

– Mandi Stanley

252. **When we are clearer on what makes up our own recipe for happiness, we will find ourselves saying with satisfaction, "It doesn't get any better than this."**

– Linda Edgecombe

253. **Take back control of your time.** Robert J. Hastings once said that the great dividing line between success and failure can be expressed in five words: *I did not have time!*

– David G. Lewis

254. Being a good person is no guarantee of entrepreneurial success. **Success requires hard work, accumulated knowledge you put to use in making great decisions, the support of people who can help you in significant ways, and a customer base that thinks you are the greatest supplier of whatever it is you sell.**

– Doug Smart

255. **Surround yourself with positive people.** People who are helpful, supportive, enthusiastic, truthful, and optimistic will help you a lot more than people who are the opposite.

– Donna Satchell

256. **Focus on the positive, smile through the negative, and keep pushing ahead toward what you want to accomplish.**

– DJ Harrington

257. Your goals may change as you change. **Adjust your life goals regularly to reflect your growth, life situations and needs. The process of goal setting is designed to help you.**

– Mike Monahan

258. **Present yourself as a confident person.**

– Mandi Stanley

259. **Act like a winner even if you are losing.** I've coached plenty of CEOs who privately feel like imposters. They're not and neither are you.

– Connie Dieken

260. **Maintain perspective.** Life is a series of ups and downs, successes and failures.

– Robert Stack

261. **Believe in yourself.** If you don't, who else will?

– Kafi Matimiloju

262. When you share your dreams with your friends and they tell you that you are out of your mind, don't change your dreams. **Change your friends.**

– Greg Maciolek

263. **Celebrate your small and large successes, even if you are alone at the celebration.** If others are too busy, not interested, or preoccupied with their own concerns, do not let that stop you from celebrating your achievements. Take yourself out for dinner, treat yourself to a day at a spa, buy yourself a gift, or celebrate by doing something special.

– Donna Satchell

264. **Stop wasting time!** No one has ever won an award for procrastination.

– David G. Lewis

265. **Tomorrow is already here.** Improve your batting average. Learn from yesterday and implement as if your life depends on it. In many ways it does.

– Connie Dieken

266. **Be more candid.** When people are upfront with you, praise it, reward it. Let others know you value straight shooters because they make the business more idea-rich and eliminate mind-numbing meetings and cover-your-butt reports.

– Connie Dieken

267. **It's not always to your advantage to be first in line!**

– David G. Lewis

268. **For a vision to be successful, the picture has to include more people than just you.**

– Cheryl Stock

269. **Dreams and goals that address a shared value of the community are most likely to succeed.**

– Phoebe Bailey

270. **It is sometimes necessary to shed friends as you become more successful.** Why? You will change but they won't. So the old relationship will no longer exist and the new one will not be as satisfying to you or them.

– Doug Smart

271. **Goals are dreams with deadlines.**

– Greg Maciolek

272. **Reaching mutual goals takes consensus. Gain agreement about "what is so," identifying "what could be," and generating solutions that "we can get excited about supporting."**

– Sid Ridgley

273. **Be authentic.** If you're approachable, people will help you stay on track by giving you feedback that's fast and straight.

– Connie Dieken

274. **Once a month make a date with yourself and do something that makes you very happy.**

– David G. Lewis

275. **When making a public speaking presentation that concerns your goals, find a way to tie your goals to your audience's goals.** You want to make it easy for them to tie their goals with yours.

– Mandi Stanley

276. **Measure your progress for great success.** Once you set your goals, make sure you are getting the results you want. If you derail, make the necessary adjustments to your plan and quickly get back on track.

– Kafi Matimiloju

277. **No goals? No way will you reach living your dreams, unless your dreams are small.**

– Robert Stack

278. **Visualize a future in which you have fulfilled your dream.** Let this personal vision excite and inspire you. This vision will be the touchstone that sustains you on your journey.

– Phoebe Bailey

279. **Live and breathe your goals every day.** Many unsuccessful people see their goals as an "add on" in their lives. Many successful people see their goals as the core of their lives.

– DJ Harrington

280. There may be many roads leading to your goals. **If the road you are on is not getting you where you want to go, try another.**

– Mike Monahan

281. **Capture your great ideas in a journal, such as a notebook you keep next to your bed.**

– Mandi Stanley

282. **Before committing to a goal, ask yourself, "Is it specific enough?"** For example, don't just say, "I want to be happy." Instead, clearly describe what you want to do, be, or have that would make you feel happy. Then state a clear, specific goal that will help you get there.

– Connie Dieken

283. **Enthusiasm reflects confidence and inspires others to act.**

– Sid Ridgley

284. **Dress as if you have already succeeded.** This will send a visual signal to yourself and others that you and your goal belong together.

– Mandi Stanley

285. **Guard your thinking.** Earl Nightingale was wise to say, "You become what you think about." So what do you spend your time thinking about?

– Donna Satchell

286. **The first step to overcoming a fear is to take a first step.** Even if it is only a few minutes, start something today that will help you get closer to one of your goals in life. Feel the power you connect with by starting.

– *Linda Edgecombe*

287. **Passion trumps fear.** If anxiety sets in, focus on your passion to overcome your fear. Don't get caught up in the minutia of tasks—instead, remember the outcome you want to create and let your passion guide you.

– *Connie Dieken*

288. **Be a generous giver.** Those who give much, receive much. This is the Law of Reciprocity.

– *David G. Lewis*

289. **In every situation that does not go as you wanted, look for "come back" opportunities.** They are always present.

– Robert Stack

290. **Don't diminish difficult messages.** Fight the impulse to soft-pedal bad news to your team or to yourself.

– Connie Dieken

291. **Look for ways to add value to other people's lives.**

– Cheryl Stock

292. **View your friends and colleagues as allies for accomplishing your goals.**

– Sid Ridgley

293. **Well-designed goals help us:**

- Know where we're going
- Make tough decisions
- Set benchmarks for our personal achievement
- Measure our progress
- Give us a reason to celebrate achievements

– Mike Monahan

294. **Stop taking "No" from those who can't tell you "Yes."**

– Keith L. Brown

295. **We learn more from our mistakes then we learn from our successes.**

– Doug Smart

296. **Take care of your health while you pursue your goals.** Maintaining good health is not something you can put off until later.

– Mandi Stanley

297. **Set "stretch goals" along with your regular goals.** "Stretch goals" are those aspirations you have that are not easy to achieve. Others may call them unrealistic. Oftentimes, many of our goals are too achievable and are more like activities on a "to do" list. Push yourself to a higher level than you think you can obtain. Amaze yourself.

– Donna Satchell

298. **Tell your best friend what you are going to accomplish in the next 30 days.** The point is to feel accountable to someone else. No excuses accepted!

– Linda Edgecombe

299. **When your current reality isn't living up to your expectations, take stock, make necessary adjustments, restate your goals, set new priorities, and move on.**

– David G. Lewis

300. **Allow for adventures you cannot imagine at the onset of your journey to fulfilling your dreams.**

– Phoebe Bailey

301. **In the final analysis, you alone are responsible for reaching or not reaching your goals.**

– DJ Harrington

302. **Persist and take your goals to completion.** Finish what you start! It is easy to start a journey, but only those that persist get to the finish line and earn the rewards.

– Kafi Matimiloju

303. Help others to achieve their goals by being a coach, mentor, and cheerleader. **What you give of yourself, expecting nothing in return, you will receive back ten-fold.**

– Greg Maciolek

*"You are never too old
to set another goal or
to dream a new dream."*

— Les Brown

*"Let me tell you
the secret that has
led me to my goal:
my strength lies solely
in my tenacity."*

— Louis Pasteur

"Man is a goal seeking animal. His life only has meaning if he is reaching out and striving for his goals."

— Aristotle

"My philosophy of life is that if we make up our mind what we are going to make of our lives, then work hard toward that goal, we never lose – somehow we win out."

— Ronald Reagan

Contributors

Phoebe Bailey

Through motivational speeches, seminars and workshops, Phoebe moves audiences from theory to practice in building community, increasing effectiveness, and recapturing the joy of a life committed to growth and development. Her messages reflect the hard lessons learned on the frontline as teacher, trainer, and public school administrator.

Contact Information:
Phoebe L. Bailey, Ph.D.
Visions in Action USA
955 Juniper Street NE, Suite 4130
Atlanta, GA 30309
Phone: (404) 892-9066
E-mail: drbailey@VisionsInActionUSA.com
Website: www.VisionsInActionUSA.com

CSP, *Certified Speaking Professional*, is the highest earned designation of the National Speakers Association.

Keith L. Brown

Called the "Motivator of the Millennium," Keith helps people move from living under supervision to manifesting a SUPER-VISION. His keynotes and workshops inspire and empower education, corporate, government, and faith-based organizations. Keith is the author of *CHITLINS [Creative Helpful Intuitive Thoughts Lifting Individuals Naturally Seeking]* and co-author of *Conversations on Success*. He and his lovely wife, Wakea, are proud parents of one sensational son, Keon.

Contact Information:

Keith L. Brown
20/20 Enterprises
115 Courtney's Lane
Fayetteville, GA 30215
Phone: (770) 460-5679
Toll-free: (800) 725-2694, pin 0726
E-mail: KeithSpeaks@KeithLBrown.com
Website: www.KeithLBrown.com

Linda Edgecombe, CSP

Linda is an internationally known humorous speaker, trainer and consultant. The *Wall Street Journal* has quoted her as an expert on shifting perspectives. Linda shows audiences how they can shift their perspectives on life, work and themselves. Her message is as welcome as a deep belly laugh and as profound as an honest look in the mirror.

Contact Information:

Linda Edgecombe, CSP
Learning Edge Resources
2770 Reyn Road
Kelowna, British Columbia V1V 2G7
Phone: (250) 868-9601
Toll-free: (888) 868-9601
E-mail: LindaEdgecombe@shaw.ca
Website: www.LindaEdgecombe.com

Connie Dieken

Connie Dieken helps organizations build buy-in through influential communication. She is a 5-time Emmy® Award winner and inductee in the Radio & Television Broadcasters Hall of Fame. Connie teaches how to cut through CommuniClutter™ with clarity, and influence customers and staff to trigger commitment and powerful results. She is a co-author of *Communicate Clearly, Confidently & Credibly*.

Contact Information:

Connie Dieken
onPoint™ Communication
32818 Walker Road, #298
Avon Lake, OH 44012
Phone: (440) 930-8500
Toll-free: (800) 505-9480
E-mail: Connie@onPointComm.com
Website: www.onPointComm.com

DJ Harrington, CSP

DJ has provided companies worldwide with marketing and telephone skills designed to enhance their telephone and customer service techniques. He teaches the EMS formula for guaranteed success: *educate*, *motivate*, and carry *solutions*. He is a nationally recognized author, journalist, seminar leader and marketing consultant.

Contact Information:

DJ Harrington, CSP
Phone Logic, Inc.
2189 Cleveland Street, Suite 257
Clearwater, FL 33765
Toll-free: (800) 352-5252
E-mail: DJHarrington@tune2.tv

David G. Lewis

David is an energetic speaker who uses his personal experience to motivate and teach people how to make sense of a world that often seems senseless. He speaks at conferences and conventions across North America. He teaches Political Science at Heartland College.

Contact Information:

David G. Lewis
Lewis Consulting Group, Inc.
1701 E. Empire Street, Suite 360 #146
Bloomington, IL 61704
Phone: (309) 827-0540
E-mail: David@DavidGLewis.com
Website: www.DavidGLewis.com

Greg Maciolek

As a consultant and speaker, Greg helps organizations increase profits by increasing productivity and decreasing employee turnover. He does this through leadership development at the senior level and working with executive teams to be more effective. He uses employee assessments for hiring, promoting and developing employees. He has served as a fighter pilot and flying commander responsible for 1,100 members.

Contact Information:

Greg Maciolek
Integrated Management Resources, Inc.
P.O. Box 31933
Knoxville, TN 37930-1933
Phone: (865) 539-3700
Toll-free: (800) 262-6403
E-mail: Greg.Maciolek@imrtn.com
Website: www.IntegratedManagementResources.com

Kafi Matimiloju

An international speaker, trainer, and consultant, Kafi has spent sixteen years working with Fortune 1000 organizations supporting projects that require the successful integration of people, processes and technology. Formerly a shy and reserved business professional who loathed networking, Kafi beat her fear and now enjoys power networking. Her motto, "Be memorable and leave a lasting impression!" Kafi leads self-improvement seminars that are interactive, informative, and fun.

Contact Information:

Kafi Matimiloju
KiSoBo, Inc.
P.O. Box 19957
Atlanta, GA 30325
Phone: (678) 797-0369
E-mail: Kafi@KiSoBo.com
Website: www.KiSoBo.com

Mike Monahan

Mike's expertise is in helping teams and individuals improve performance, with special focus on the human side of change. Mike conducts leader and manager competency development sessions and has a series of customizable training interventions for all levels of supervisors and managers. He is a co-author of *Where There's Change There's Opportunity, Irresistible Leadership, Thriving in the Midst of Change,* and all six volumes of the *Insights from Experts* Series.

Contact Information:

Mike Monahan
Healthcare Resources Associates
8505 S. Newcombe Court, Suite A
Littleton, CO 80127
Phone and Fax: (303) 948-1587
Toll-free: (800) 759-2881
E-mail: M2HRA@aol.com

Sid Ridgley, CSP

As an organizational development specialist and professional speaker, Sid advises leaders in their pursuit of creating organizational workplaces that are customer and employee centered. His areas of expertise are customer satisfaction and loyalty, sales, leadership development, and front-line driven cultural change processes.

Contact Information:

Sid Ridgley, MBA, CSP
Simul Corporation
23 Fry Court
Markham, Ontario L3P 4G9
Phone: (905) 294-1260
Toll-free: (888) 291-7892
E-mail: SRidgley@SimulCorp.com
Website: www.SimulCorp.com

Donna Satchell

Donna works with individuals who want to achieve remarkable success and businesses that want strong teams that serve their customers exceptionally well. In addition, she teaches public speaking skills. Her company name, STARR is an acronym for Speeches, Training, Assessments, Resources and Results, which are the deliverables her business provides across North America.

Contact Information:

Donna Satchell
STARR Consulting & Training LLC
6304 Southland Forest Drive
Stone Mountain, GA 30087
Phone: (770) 498-0400
E-mail: Donna@STARRct.com
Website: www.STARRct.com

Doug Smart , CSP

Doug Smart helps people work smart and live happy. He has expertise in helping organizations select, develop, and retain top talent. He is the author of the book, *Sell Smarter, Faster & Easier by Understanding Your Buyer's Personality Profile*. Doug is frequently invited to speak at conferences and conventions.

Contact Information:

Doug Smart, CSP
Smart Business, Inc.
PO Box 768024
Roswell, GA 30076
Phone: (770) 587-9784
Toll-free: (800) 299-3737
E-mail: Doug@DougSmart.com
Website: www.DougSmart.com

Robert Stack

As a professional development coach, Robert is dedicated to improving the quality of life for others who face life's not so funny stuff. He specializes in personal reputation management and coaches individuals as well as organizations on how to transform adversity into opportunity. He is co-author of *Success is a Journey*.

Contact Information:

Robert Stack, CLC, APR, Fellow PRSA
COMEBACK LLC
4521 PGA Blvd.
Palm Beach Gardens, FL 33418
Phone: (561) 776-0101
Toll-free: (866) 666-6064
E-mail: Robert@ComebackCoach.com
Website: www.ComebackCoach.com

Cheryl Stock

Cheryl works with people who want more energy, direction and passion in their lives and results from their businesses. Her expertise is in communication and presentation skills, marketing, leadership and achieving higher accomplishment levels. In 2003, Cheryl was named "Trainer of the Year" by the Non-Profit Resource Center. As one client says, "She'll rock you with her energy. She is contagious!"

Contact Information:

Cheryl Stock
C. Stock & Associates, Inc.
P.O. Box 25355
Sarasota, FL 34277
Phone: (941) 346-3624
E-mail: Cheryl@CherylStock.com
Website: www.CherylStock.com

Mandi Stanley, CSP

Mandi works with business leaders who want to boost their professional image and with people who want to be better speakers and writers. Her signature seminars are *"Hair-On-Fire!" Presentation Skills, 7½ Ways To Wake Up Your Writing,* and *Proof It: How To Be A Better Proofreader.* All are designed to help participants get their messages across and achieve the results they want.

Contact Information:

Mandi Stanley, CSP
429 Cherry Hill Drive
Madison, MS 39110
Phone: (601) 856-8282
E-mail: Mandi@MandiStanley.com
Website:www.MandiStanley.com